A Church on JARROM STREET:

150 years of St Andrew's Church, Leicester

Paul Griffiths

KAIROS PRESS

in association with
St Andrew's Church
Jarrom Street
Leicester

2012

ISBN 978-1-871344-32-5

Design and Layout by Robin Stevenson, Kairos Press
Body text in Times New Roman 11pt
Printed in Great Britain by Barkers Printers, Leicester

Front Cover. St Andrew's Church, Jarrom Street from the east. Photograph by Robin Stevenson, 2012.

Back cover: The sanctuary of St Andrew's, Jarrom Street. Photograph by Canon Barry Naylor, 2011.

Published in Great Britain by
KAIROS PRESS

in association with
St Andrew's Church,
Jarrom Street,
Leicester
LE2 7DH

Contents

Acknowledgements

Many people have helped me to research and write this history but I owe a particular debt to Geoff Brandwood, the Chambers family, Alan Christopher, Marian Coom, Neil Crutchley, Jean Davis, Richard Gill, David Gillman, John Howard, Tom Ipgrave and Elisabeth Sutherland. I am also grateful to Robin Stevenson for his advice and care in arranging publication.

My efforts would have ceased long ago, however, had it not been for the encouragement of Fr Barry Naylor and the present congregation at St Andrew's. They have given generously of their time and knowledge. I am particularly grateful to the members of the 'History Group' - Monica Clowes, Wendy Commons, Neville Iliffe, Don Sherriff and Mary Watts – and have very much valued their enthusiasm and friendship over recent months. I hope they will feel that the result is worthy of the Church which they have served for so many years.

Paul Griffiths
Leicester
March 2012

I am grateful to Richard Gill for permission to reproduce his poem and to Marian Coom for permission to quote the description of her father's early life at St Andrew's. The illustrations have come from a variety of sources and I have acknowledged these in the accompanying text.

Foreword

This booklet, written by Paul Griffiths, speaks of the history of St Andrew's Church, Jarrom Street, of its role as a place of Catholic worship in the Church of England and its service to the community between 1862 and 2012.

The church stands at a significant cross-roads between De Montfort University and the Royal Infirmary. There have been many changes to the local area over the last 150 years, not least the demolition of hundreds of houses as well as shops and schools, to be replaced by the present university and the hospital. The ministry of St Andrew's has developed over the decades with renowned parish priests ministering, often for many years, and being much loved. St Andrew's has also been blessed by lay people down the generations who have given so generously of their time, their money and their skills in the service of the Gospel. Without them the Church would not be standing today.

St Andrew's is now the home to a variety of expressions of ministry, making the most of the facilities offered by the beautiful and spacious Church and its newly refurbished Hall, using them to witness to the transforming power of the Gospel in this part of Leicester. The Church seeks to develop relationships with our rich diversity of neighbours using the wonderful buildings to witness to God's boundless generosity and the power of his love to transform.

The centrality of the Mass to the life of St Andrew's affirms the desire both to worship God at the Altar and to serve the One whom we encounter there in those who live, work and study in the area, in those who use the Church and the Community Hall for a wide variety of purposes and in those who pass by, day by day, going about their daily business or off to enjoy matches at the local sports stadia.

St. Andrew's, Jarrom Street, has stood as a beacon of faith for 150 years and, building on the traditions of the past, we live in the reality of the present and look to the future radiating Gospel hope.

Canon Barry Naylor
Urban Canon and Parish Priest
March 2012

St Andrew's, Jarrom Street, Leicester

One grey November Sunday afternoon
The year I came to Leicester – '66 –
I took a walk down terraced streets, which soon
Would be bulldozed to heaps of slates and bricks,
When in the dereliction of that scene
I came upon a church's gaunt east end –
An apse with narrow windows, shafts between,
The walls a dark, polychromatic blend,
Intensely zig-zagged, blue upon red,
And triple bell-cote etched against the sky.
The textures of those smoke stained bricks all said:
"We have the look of churches that are high".
The formal service board in solemn black
Confirmed it all: the early mass at eight,
And by the door, fixed with a single tack,
Prayers for departed priests associate,
Of Walsingham. I cranked the gothic door,
Inhaled the spicy aromatic smell,
Made out encaustic tiles upon the floor,
And felt the vastness of the giant shell.
Then, as the darkness thinned, I caught the sight
Of candle stands, of saints, of sanctus bell
And one bright flame that burned with flesh-hued light.

Richard Gill

Chapter 1
1862: Beginnings

St Andrew's was born at a time of great change in Leicester. The town was expanding rapidly and from a population of less than 17,000 in 1801, it had quadrupled to 68,000 by 1861. In 1801, almost everyone lived within the line of the ancient walls; by 1861, the town was advancing into the surrounding countryside.

At first, most building took place to the east and northeast, attracted by the canal, the turnpike road and ready supplies of building land. Little happened to the south. There was some 'ribbon' development along Horse Pool Street (now Oxford Street) and Grange Lane towards the Infirmary but the South Fields stood in the way of further building. These were fields over which the Freemen of Leicester held grazing rights. An Act of Parliament to enclose the Fields was passed in 1804 but most of the land was allocated to the Corporation and was only slowly released for building. Initially, plots were sold for high quality housing between Welford Road and New Walk.

Only later was much land released to the west of Oxford Street. Development here waited until the 1850s and 1860s and the emphasis was then on terraced housing for poorer people, interspersed with small factories and warehouses. By 1857, development stretched from the Newarke to Napier Street (now beneath the Infirmary) and soon afterwards it reached Walnut Street. This area was to become the heart of St Andrew's parish.

For centuries, the Church of England had served Leicester from the five medieval churches which survived the Reformation – All Saints, St Margaret, St Martin, St Mary de Castro, and St Nicholas. Since then, Dissenters, especially Baptists and Independents, had flourished in the town and had built a variety of chapels and meeting rooms. Indeed, Leicester became known as a Non-conformist stronghold, a reputation it retained into the twentieth century.

As the town started to expand in the nineteenth century, it became clear that the five medieval churches were inadequate. Nationally too, there was concern about the low level of churchgoing amongst the new urban populations and the 'threat' of Non-conformity. If the Church of England was to maintain its witness and role in national life, it had to have a visible presence in the new communities and provide more places for people to worship.

The first practical response in Leicester was the building of St George's Church on Rutland Street, to the east of the town, between 1823 and 1827. It was (and still is) a massive stone structure, designed originally to seat 2,000 worshippers and paid for nationally by the Church Building Commissioners. It was followed by two more modest brick churches both funded locally. Christ Church, off Wharf Street, was completed in 1839 and seated 1,200 people. Holy Trinity was consecrated in 1840 and served the first developments on the South Fields, the high class streets around Regent Road. At first, Holy Trinity was a simple unadorned Church; only in the 1870s did it acquire the elaborate decoration which it now displays.

After Holy Trinity, church building in Leicester paused. Not until the 1850s was another new church commissioned and, by then, the Church of England had been deeply stirred by fresh ideas about its role and purpose. Aligned to these were new fashions in architecture. Both were to affect St Andrew's profoundly.

The new ideas were those of the Oxford Movement. This was 'ignited' by John Keble in a sermon preached in 1833 and, over the next few years, the leaders of the Movement developed their ideas in a series of Tracts (so that supporters were often known as "Tractarians"). Proponents sought to renew the Church of England by stressing its Catholic roots. They looked to the faith and practice of the English church in medieval times, prior to the introduction of Protestant ideas at the Reformation. The Movement attracted much hostility and suspicion for a good part of the nineteenth century.

However, it soon found ready allies in the world of architecture. Here, A.W.N. Pugin was also extolling the virtues of medieval times and, in particular, of medieval Gothic architecture. He went as far as to claim that Gothic was the only acceptable style for Christian churches. Pugin's followers embraced his ideas with enthusiasm and formed the Ecclesiological Society to promote them. The Society had forthright views about the proper appearance and layout of churches and one of its favoured architects was George Gilbert Scott.

Opposite: A Leicester Vista: painting by Norman Ernest Ellis (1913-1971). St Andrew's is just to the left of this view, which depicts the area before the Clean Air Acts, and the post-war clearance and redevelopment.

Tractarians stressed the centrality of the Eucharist (Holy Communion) in Christian life and worship, as had been the case in medieval times. This, they thought, should be reflected in church buildings; a church's structure, layout and design ought to focus attention on the altar and allow space for the liturgy surrounding the Eucharist to be performed with dignity.

This was in contrast to most churches of the day where pre-eminence was given to preaching. Hearing 'the word' was vital and, as a consequence, the focus of the church was the pulpit. The Eucharist was celebrated infrequently and could be accommodated in a short chancel. This was the pattern adopted by Leicester's new churches in the 1820s and 1830s and is still evident in the layout of Holy Trinity today.

By 1851, the population of Leicester had grown to over 61,000. The Church of England's provision was still woefully inadequate, with just 8 churches and 16 clergy serving the town. Concerned and wealthy individuals in the county decided to act and formed a Church Extension Fund (CEF) in 1851. Subscribers were asked to commit funds for 3 or 5 years, with the main objective being the creation of new churches and schools in "overgrown parishes".

At first, the Fund focused on St George's parish. It granted £2,700 towards the cost of purchasing land and building the Church of St John the Divine on Ashwell Street. The foundation stone was laid in 1853 and the Church consecrated 18 months later.

The Fund's next major project was in the parish of St Mary de Castro. The Vicar and Churchwardens of St Mary's had approached it about the area south of Mill Lane which was expanding rapidly and was already home to at least 5,000 souls. *"Nearly the whole population are either framework knitters, loom weavers, employed in factories, mechanics, or small shop-keepers; and ... as such, they are able to render but little, if any assistance to the object in view"* (i.e. the building and endowment of a new church). As a temporary measure, the Vicar and his *"indefatigable"* curates were holding services in two schoolrooms but it was impossible for him to do more *"from the smallness of the income of the living and the many other demands of a parochial nature"*.[1]

The CEF's Committee was evidently sympathetic and, in March 1860, it increased an earlier offer of grant to £2,900. This was conditional on an equal sum being raised from voluntary contributions and other sources. By this stage, the Committee must have been confident because, at the same meeting, it approved the purchase of a site at the corner of Jarrom Street and Asylum

Street (now Gateway Street) and agreed plans submitted by the architect, George Gilbert Scott.

The CEF played a major role in focusing efforts to build St Andrew's, as well as providing a substantial proportion of the funds. Its Secretary at the time was Canon William Fry. Contemporary (and later) accounts acknowledge his energy and leadership in the creation of St John's, St Andrew's and, later, St Matthew's Churches and Schools but the exact nature of his role is difficult to uncover. One account from 1904 suggests that Canon Fry acted *"to a great extent independently"*[2] in originating the appeal for funds at St Andrew's. He is also known to have bought land on his own initiative at times and this seems to have been the case, at least, for the Laxton and Knighton Street Schools. His concern did not end with the building of St Andrew's and its Schools; in 1864, he organised a bazaar lasting four days to raise funds for a vicarage.

The role of the CEF is likely to explain the choice of architect for St Andrew's and the ideas behind its design. The CEF 'sponsored' the building of three new churches in Leicester and, in each case, the architect was George Gilbert Scott. The Committee was evidently satisfied with his work at St John the Divine and, since then, he had carried out restoration work on other churches in the town and the surrounding area. Based in London, Scott had a national reputation and could be relied upon to produce designs in line with 'modern' ideas. It is significant that St John's, St Andrew's and St Matthew's were all Gothic designs based on Ecclesiological principles. For example, they gave prominence to the altar rather than the pulpit and had sizeable chancels and high pitched open roofs.

At St Andrew's, the foundation stone was laid by the Duke of Rutland in December 1860. The builders, Osborn Brothers, worked quickly and the church was consecrated on 20th February 1862. As the Bishop of Peterborough was indisposed, the ceremony was performed by the Bishop of Sodor and Man. According to the "Leicester Journal", local people would no longer be *"pushed into a dark corner under a gallery, while the comfortable seats in the nave are reserved for the more aristocratic worshippers"*. Instead, *"they have now a building in which, in appearance at least, no distinction is made between the rich and the poor, and in which they may feel that they are cared for, and welcome"*.[3]

A new parish of more than 5,000 people was carved out of the existing parish of St Mary de Castro and the first Vicar appointed.

Chapter 2
The Building

To the townsfolk of Leicester in 1862, St Andrew's must have seemed a striking, even shocking, building, especially for a church. It was far more surprising than Scott's first church in the town, St John the Divine, which had been built in stone and used familiar medieval forms. At St Andrew's, in contrast, Scott employed the Gothic style in radically new ways. In accepting his designs, the CEF's Committee ventured that *"it would be a bold structure, very much out of the common way"*.[4]

Firstly, St Andrew's was built in brick. This was common for Non-conformist chapels but unusual at the time for Leicestershire churches. Christ Church and Holy Trinity had set precedents but their brickwork was plain and orderly. At St Andrew's, the exterior brick is bright red and decorated with blue brick in bands and geometric patterns. Inside, buff bricks predominate but they are set with lively patterns in red and blue. St Andrew's was one of the first buildings in Leicester to illustrate the delights of 'polychrome' brickwork and amongst the earliest churches in the country to do so.

Secondly, Scott created a huge space inside St Andrew's. His basic plan is cruciform with a wide nave, two prominent transepts and a chancel with a rounded (apsidal) end. Attached to the south wall is a substantial porch. The nave is enclosed beneath a single steeply pitched roof, its powerful wooden ribs springing from shafts on the walls, at a height of about 12 feet, to a ridge almost 60 feet above the floor. Outside, the chancel arch projects above the roof line to give a simple bellcote with three openings.

There are no aisles, no projecting chapels and no tower or spire. Apart from the polychrome brickwork, there is little ornamentation. The windows are lancets or simple roundels; they are punched through the brickwork to give the impression of plate tracery and are not framed with mouldings or other decoration. The original furnishings were plain and intended not to

Opposite: St Andrew's Church, Leicester. An engraving from Building News, 28th February 1862. Apart from the loss of some finials, it could be 2012.

Engraving of St Andrew's, Jarrom Street, from Building News, 28th February 1862.

detract from the boldness of the huge shell and its patterned brickwork. The building speaks through its size and structure and through the spaces it creates and shelters under its great roof.

At the consecration in 1862, the "Leicester Journal" declared:

> *"The view presented on entering the church at the west door is strikingly beautiful, the rich soft colour of the bricks ... and the lofty arches which divide the nave from the chancel and the transepts, together with the complicated timbers of the roof, adding much to the general effect."*[5]

The nave construction was of particular interest to contemporaries. The Leicester Archaeological and Historical Society reported that: *"as an experiment testing the adaptation of brick in the erection of an ecclesiastical edifice without internal piers, [it] is worthy of the closest inspection and scrutiny."*[6] By spanning a wide nave with one roof, Scott had dispensed with the expense of pillars and had given a clear view of the altar and pulpit from all parts of the Church.

St Andrew's was a comparatively cheap building. It was constructed at a cost of about £5,000 and provided seats for 960 people, including benches for children in the transepts. Scott's enduring legacy was to produce a Church which could be easily adapted over the years. Its uncluttered interior has accommodated many changes; over time, it provided space for a more elaborate liturgy; it allowed the chancel to be transformed into a spacious sanctuary; it permitted the choir and organ to move between the east and west ends; it offered accommodation for chapels in the transepts; and it permitted a parish room to be built alongside the nave.

Sir George Gilbert Scott (1811-1878) was the most prolific of Victorian architects. He designed buildings, almost all in the Gothic Revival style, across Britain and abroad. One biographer describes 879 projects but insists that this list is not exhaustive (and notes that some plans were not executed). For the people of Leicester, Scott's Midland Grand Hotel at St Pancras station, built a few years after St Andrew's, is probably his most memorable work. Others may know the Albert Memorial, also in London, and Kelham Hall near Newark. Scott employed numerous assistants to cope with the volume of work and several later became famous in their own right. According to architectural critics, the quality of work emanating from Scott's office ranged from dull to brilliant.

Churches and cathedrals formed a large part of Scott's output both as new buildings and as major restorations of medieval buildings. However,

Leicester was exceptional for a town of its size in boasting four new churches by Scott. St Andrew's, St John's and St Matthew's were all built in the 1850s and 1860s under the auspices of the CEF; St Saviour's in Spinney Hills was a late work and completed in 1877, the year before his death. Of the four, only St Andrew's remains as a 'working' church. St Matthews has been demolished and St John's converted into flats, whilst regular services at St Saviour's ceased in 2006.

St Andrew's is not a typical Scott church. Rather it belongs to a small group of designs, completed in the late 1850s and early 1860s, which makes extensive use of polychrome brickwork. The English Heritage listing gives three others – Crewe Green in Cheshire, Ottershaw in Surrey and St Andrew's at Uxbridge in west London. To these, St Matthew's at Yiewsley, also in west London, is usually added although Scott's Church there now forms only part of a much larger building. It is tempting to speculate that this group of churches was the work of one assistant in Scott's office although Scott himself presumably approved the broad idea.

St Michael's at Crewe Green is a particularly delightful 'cousin' of St Andrew's. It is smaller and without transepts but, like St Andrew's, displays bold polychrome brickwork both inside and out. The chancel also terminates in a semicircular apse with a similar roof structure and lancet windows. However, St Michael's shows the benefits of having a wealthy patron; it is much more richly decorated than St Andrew's and is adorned with a small tower and spire.

Scott's use of polychromy in this group of churches is reminiscent of another Victorian architect, William Butterfield (1814-1900). Between 1850 and 1859, Butterfield built a Church and associated buildings on Margaret Street in central London to the requirements of the Ecclesiological Society and, as intended, All Saints' became a model for the design of new churches in urban areas. Its exterior is in polychrome brick from top to bottom.

Chapter 3
1862 – 1912: Growth

The Reverend John Spittal was 29 when he was made Vicar of St Andrew's in 1862. A Scotsman from a prosperous Edinburgh family, he had served two brief curacies in east London before moving to Leicester. He faced the daunting task of building up the life of the Church in a parish where most of the 5,000 or more inhabitants had arrived recently and were struggling to earn a living.

There were some foundations on which to build. Church Schools were already operating at Paradise Place (off Oxford Street), Laxton Street and Knighton Street and a fourth, the Victoria School, was to open on Deacon Street in 1865. As a temporary measure, the clergy of St Mary de Castro had been organising Sunday services in the Laxton Street schoolroom and a Wednesday evening service at Paradise Place. This approach to new parishes was typical of Canon Fry, the CEF Secretary; he would encourage mission meetings in schools in advance of the opening of a church, with the intention of creating the core of a new congregation.

Once opened, St Andrew's began to acquire the 'necessities' of an English Victorian church. In 1864, a curate arrived. In 1865, the Vicarage, also designed by George Gilbert Scott, was completed. Later that year, an organ was installed in the Church to replace the harmonium. A choir was formed and, in 1866, the first magazine was published.

A pattern of services also developed. By the end of 1866, the congregation could expect four services on a Sunday – Holy Communion at 8am, Morning Prayer at 10.30am, the Litany and a lecture at 3pm and Evening Prayer at 6.30pm. Shorter morning and evening prayers were also said on weekdays, with a sermon added on Wednesday evenings. An extra celebration of Holy Communion took place at noon on the first Sunday of each month and, from 1867, this was a choral occasion. Also in 1867, Holy Communion was offered on major Saints' Days at 8am. The increasing frequency of Communion, which had begun on a monthly basis in 1862, is significant and is an indication of Fr Spittal's Tractarian sympathies.

The early emphasis at St Andrew's was on teaching and outreach. In 1866, morning and afternoon Sunday Schools were advertised at three locations – Knighton Street, Laxton Street and Deacon Street – and a class for Sunday School teachers and helpers met on Saturday evenings. In January 1868, the magazine reported a shortage of teachers and appealed for more volunteers. The annual Sunday School 'Treat' was already a highlight of the year. In 1869, for example, 100 older scholars and 60 teachers and friends enjoyed an afternoon at Bradgate. On the following day, 900 of the younger pupils marched to Freemens Pasture for games and amusements, later returning to Laxton Street School for tea and musical entertainment.

The practice of holding Mission meetings in schools continued and expanded. At a peak in 1866, five evening meetings per week were listed using three schoolrooms. Variously described as 'Meetings for Bible Exposition and Prayer' and 'Mission Services and Lectures', they seem to have been less formal than services in Church and with a greater teaching element. Ultimately, however, they were intended to swell the congregation at St Andrew's. A group of young men from the Church was commended in December 1866 for its dedication in conducting meetings at Paradise Place and visiting the poor of that district.

Of the early organisations attached to the Church, three deserve comment. The Young Men's Mutual Improvement Society features prominently in the magazine. Founded in 1865, it met weekly at Deacon Street School, its chief object being *"the mental culture of its members."*[7] By 1868, it could boast 111 current members, a programme of discussions and debates, regular entertainment evenings, a library, a cricket team and a band. Less ambitious, but still in the 'self help' tradition, was the Sewing Meeting. In 1866, this was reported to attract 60 to 80 women to its weekly meeting. Further volunteers were sought to 'manage the sewing' and to read to the members whilst they worked. The Church also had a Penny Bank which operated in conjunction with the Leicester Savings Bank and opened for an hour each Monday. A motto on the passbook declared: *"For age and want save what you may. To be happy tomorrow, be careful today."*

Fr Spittal's Tractarian views on Holy Communion have already been noted. They were also evident in the decoration of the altar at St Andrew's, the general reverence of the services and the 'eastward position' of the priest when celebrating Communion. Although these seem small matters today they were of great significance to the Victorians and could attract much hostility in some circles.

Leicester was not fertile ground for the Tractarians and Fr Spittal's stance was a lonely one. Only at St Margaret's were there sympathetic ears. Tractarian ideas had been introduced here by the Reverend William Anderdon; he was Vicar from 1846 but had left after four years to join the Roman Catholic Church. His successor continued the Tractarian approach but cautiously. St Margaret's and St Andrew's shared the task of hosting meetings of the Leicester branch of the English Church Union, an organisation set up to promote and defend the ideas of the Oxford Movement. For St Andrew's, this produced visits from leading national figures such as Fr Charles Lowder in 1872 and Fr Arthur Stanton in 1874.

No other church in Leicester took up the Tractarian cause until St Paul's was opened in the Westcotes area in 1871. Under its Vicar of 40 years, the Reverend James Mason, it became the 'beacon' of Tractarianism in Leicester and much information about the Movement's early days is contained in its Jubilee history of 1921. It records that both Fr Mason and Fr Spittal offered the sacrament of confession, probably the most contentious of the Tractarian practices. Such was the strength of feeling against confession that a crowded meeting was organised in the Temperance Hall in April 1874 to protest against its use by the two priests. In the event, the organisers' case was greatly weakened when a Non-conformist minister, expected to be highly critical of the practice, could only praise Fr Mason's piety.

By then, however, Fr Spittal was about to leave St Andrew's for a new post in Oxfordshire. He was replaced by the Reverend Robert Guinness.

Few records survive of Fr Guinness's time at St Andrew's. He seems to have been a popular preacher, if judged by attendances when he returned as a guest in later years. He also appears as an early advocate of the ministry of Lay Readers. Three appointments were made at St Andrew's in 1877, only four years after their introduction in Peterborough Diocese. By 1880, there were still only two other churches in Leicester with Lay Readers and only 40 such appointments in the whole Diocese (which included Northamptonshire and Rutland as well as Leicestershire). At St Andrew's, Lay Readers seem to have played a major part in the Mission meetings.

Fr Guinness was the first Vicar of St Andrew's to be appointed as part-time Chaplain to the Leicester Royal Infirmary. He took up the post in 1878 and served for about three years, until funds became available for a

Opposite: The Church interior in the early twentieth century.
Note the chancel decoration and the elaborate altar furnishings.

Photograph provided by John Howard

full-time appointment. The Reverend Samuel Godber, formerly Curate at St Peter's Church, Highfields, then took over.

After 10 years at St Andrew's, Fr Guinness left in 1885 to become Vicar of Market Harborough. His successor at the Infirmary, Samuel Godber, became his successor at St Andrew's. The Infirmary position reverted to being part-time and Fr Godber held both posts for the next 14 years. He did so with the help of curates – and it was often said that those curates found their wives amongst the nursing staff at the Infirmary! Fr Godber was Chaplain when the Infirmary Chapel opened in 1888 and, after he died, a window was dedicated in his memory.

The parish continued to grow. The population was estimated at 10,000 by 1881, making it the fourth most populous in Leicester. An unofficial religious census, conducted by the "Leicester Mercury", gives a 'snapshot' of church attendance at the time. On 20th November 1881, it reported the following attendances at St Andrew's:

Morning	302
Afternoon	125
Evening	427

The evening Mission meetings recorded a further 72 people at Laxton Street and 58 at Knighton Street. Some people would have been counted at more than one service but, using a standard formula to take account of this, it has been estimated that about 570 individuals, not including Sunday school pupils, attended St Andrew's on that day. This was an average attendance by Leicester church standards at the time.

After Fr Spittal's departure, no further Tractarian practices were intro-duced at St Andrew's and, from a St Paul's perspective, it became a conventional Anglican church. For instance, whereas a daily Communion service was available at St Paul's from 1883, St Andrew's offered just two celebrations a week, at 8am on Sundays and at 7am on Thursdays.

However, efforts to beautify the interior of the Church, especially the chancel, intensified at St Andrew's from the late 1880s onwards. The walls behind the altar were decorated so that angelic heads now looked down from between the tops of the windows. Sanctuary curtains were hung high behind the altar and an intricately carved and painted reredos was installed. A new lectern and a new pulpit were also acquired. Only the lighting was simplified; a large corona made by Skidmore of Coventry, perhaps the only element of ostentation in the original design, was replaced by small candelabra.

The Allen brothers at St Andrew's, c.1935.
Peter (left) as a boat boy, and John (right) as a choirboy.

In 1886, a small area of St Andrew's parish was transferred to Holy Trinity. The population soon recovered, however, as new housing began to be built to the west of Havelock Street. This was made possible by major flood protection works, undertaken by the Corporation, which included the building of new bridges at Mill Lane and Walnut Street. By 1901, the population of St Andrew's parish had almost reached 11,500. Thoughts had already turned to the possible division of the parish and the construction of a second church. A site in the south of the parish was identified in 1897 and purchased after St Andrew's raised about £1,200. This investment would bear fruit in the early years of the next century.

In December 1898, the Church was shaken when Fr Godber died suddenly of a heart attack, aged 51. Clearly a popular Vicar, a memorial fund was launched immediately with a view to building a parish room in his name. The appeal was successful and the Godber Memorial building, built in the angle between the north transept of the church and the nave, opened in November 1900.

In the meantime, the Reverend Henry Tower, a Curate of St Andrew's from 1886 to 1892, stepped into the breach and took over as Vicar in March 1899. He stayed for just over a year before being attracted away to the more prestigious post of Vicar of Holy Trinity, Windsor where he was to remain for over 40 years.

The Bishop then turned to the town of Kettering in Northamptonshire for his next three appointments. Though much smaller than Leicester, Kettering shared a similar recent history and outlook. It had grown rapidly with the expansion of the boot and shoe industry and, like Leicester, was mainly Non-conformist in religion and Liberal in politics. In both towns, the Church of England, adopting a missionary stance, was working to establish new churches in the areas of population growth. In Kettering, the lead was taken by three outstanding Rectors who, between them, served the town from 1863 until 1911; the Bishop seems to have regarded their parish as a good training ground for curates destined to work in similar urban situations.

The first of these appointees was the Reverend Frederic Llewellyn Deane who was inducted as Vicar of St Andrew's in June 1900. He had been a curate at Kettering since 1891 and had married one of the former Rector's daughters. He arrived in Leicester at the age of 31. It is evident from the magazines

Opposite: Special Occasions at St Andrew's in the 1880s and 1890s: posters from the Reverend Henry Tower's scrapbook.

S. ANDREW'S, LEICESTER.

SPECIAL SERMONS.

The Dedication of the New Reredos.

THURSDAY, JULY 5th, 8 p.m. *Preacher*

Rev. P. T. BAINBRIGGE,
Vicar of St. Thomas, Regent Street, London.

SUNDAY, JULY 8th, Morning, 11 a.m. *Preacher*

Rev. D. W. PEREGRINE.

Afternoon, 3 p.m.,

A CANTATA
Founded on the Words of Bunyan's Famous Allegory,
I WILL BE SUNG BY THE CHOIR.

A SHORT ADDRESS will be given by the REV S. GODBER.

Evening, 6-30. *Preacher*

Rev. CANON INGRAM.

The Offertory will go towards paying off the Church Debt.

C. W. KILBY, Printer, &c. Belvoir Street, Leicester.

S. ANDREW'S STRING ✠ BAND.

SMOKING CONCERT

Laxton Street School,

THURSDAY, JAN. 8, 1891

AT 8 P.M.

ADMISSION 6d.

Tickets can be obtained from Rev. H. TOWER, S. Andrew's Vicarage; from the Secretary, Mr. A. HUTCHINSON, 43, Hazel Street; or from any Member of the Band.

Refreshments Provided at Moderate Charges

T. INGRAM, General Printer, 23, Hazel Street, Leicester.

S. ✠ ANDREW'S LEICESTER.

The Boys of the 1st Leicester Battalion

CHURCH LADS' BRIGADE

WILL GIVE AN

ENTERTAINMENT
IN THE

LAXTON-ST. SCHOOL
ON SHROVE TUESDAY, MARCH 1, 1892,

AT 8 P.M.

DICK WHITTINGTON

AND HIS CAT.
AND

CHRISTY MINSTRELS

Tickets: Reserved Seats, 6d. Second Seats, 3d
FUNDS URGENTLY NEEDED

T. INGRAM, Printer, &c., Hazel Street, Leicester.

S. ANDREW'S STRING BAND
WILL HOLD A

FLORAL CONVERSAZIONE
IN

LAXTON ST. SCHOOL,
ON

THURSDAY, MAY 1ST, 1890,
TO COMMENCE AT 7.30.

Mr. H. E. Quilter and Friends will EXHIBIT LIVING SPECIMENS OF POND-LIFE with Microscopes and Electric Light.

GAMES, &C. WILL BE PROVIDED.

TICKETS (including Refreshments) 1/-,
Can be obtained at S. Andrew's Vicarage, or from the Secretary, Mr. A. HUTCHINSON, 43, Hazel Street.

N.B.—IT WOULD BE APPROPRIATE FOR THE LADIES AND GENTLEMEN TO WEAR FLOWERS.

that the pace of Church life suddenly quickened. Fr Deane was clearly an energetic priest with a common touch. The number of communicants increased sharply; the Vicar became Prison Chaplain in order to pay for another curate; a Church Army Captain (complete with a harmonium on a wheelbarrow) was employed to extend the mission work; a Church Council was set up; a men's meeting was started with great success; and electric lighting was installed in the Church. Steps were also taken to renew the furnishings and fittings – for example, the pews were re-varnished, a carpet laid in the sanctuary and new coloured frontals acquired for the altar.

Actions to make the Church more attractive were accompanied by a greater emphasis on Holy Communion. This was promoted as the "chief service" and the frequency of weekday celebrations was increased. In this, Fr Deane was gently moving the congregation back to its early Tractarian roots. By now Tractarianism had developed into a broader 'Anglo-Catholic' movement and was becoming increasingly influential in the Church of England.

After four years, Fr Deane left St Andrew's to become Rector of St Mary's, Glasgow, one of the Scottish Episcopal Church's largest parochial charges. In 1908, St Mary's was hallowed as a Cathedral and Fr Deane promoted to Provost. Finally, he was consecrated as Bishop of Aberdeen and Orkney in 1917, a post he held until 1943.

Back at St Andrew's, Fr Deane was replaced by the Reverend Frederick Barré Fiest. Fr Fiest was also a former curate at Kettering and had, in fact, taken over from Fr Deane as Curate in Charge of St Mary's there. He was already well known in Leicester, having been a missioner to St Andrew's in 1903.

A major event during Fr Fiest's incumbency was the opening of a new church in St Andrew's parish. Most of the money was provided by the Nedham sisters who wished to build a church in Leicester to the memory of their parents and other family members. They were persuaded of the need at St Andrew's but were not satisfied with the land which the Church had already purchased. Instead, a more prominent site was found on Aylestone Road and an architect of national standing, George Frederick Bodley, was commissioned to design the Church. All Souls' was consecrated in June 1906. It took responsibility for a part of St Andrew's parish containing about 3,600 people; about 7,800 remained with St Andrew's.

Sadly, Fr Fiest's health was poor and, after three and a half years, he admitted that a large town parish like St Andrew's was *"beyond my strength"*.[8] He moved to be Vicar of Thurlaston, still in Leicestershire but with a population of less than 550.

The third of the 'Kettering appointments', the Reverend Alexander Sutherland Lindsay, arrived at St Andrew's in June 1908. He was the son of one of Kettering's former Rectors and had held several appointments in the Kettering area, most recently as Vicar of Desborough. He was already familiar with St Andrew's, having visited the Vicarage when his sister, Mrs Deane, lived there. Fr Lindsay guided St Andrew's through the Jubilee celebrations of 1912 and stayed until 1915 when he moved to be Vicar of Daventry. On departing, he lamented: *"I have found the work happy, but also always the master of me. It is depressing ..... to feel that the church is not really in possession of the district at all"*.[9] By now, the First World War was raging and the end of Victorian and Edwardian Britain was in sight.

A full set of St Andrew's magazines survives for the period 1897 to 1911 and shows that the Church had become a hive of activity, both social and religious. Making use of the Godber Memorial Room, the Knighton Street building and the Schools, it was home to many organisations. Prominent among them were:

- the choir,
- the Sunday School and Bible classes,
- the Church Lads' Brigade,
- the Church of England Temperance Society and the Band of Hope,
- the Men's Meeting,
- the Ladies' Working Party,
- the Scripture Union,
- the Mothers' Meeting,
- the Church Workers' Guild.

The Men's Meeting spawned an orchestral band and a Self Help Society (or 'sick club'). An Institute at Knighton Street operated as a club for men *"where everything is bright and jolly* without *the twin curse that besets so many Clubs – drinking and gambling"*[10]. It provided newspapers, games and occasional events and also organised cricket and football teams. The magazines contain references to many other groups although some were short-lived. They include boys' and girls' guilds, the gymnasium meeting, a dramatic society, a rugby club, a swimming club and a ladies' hockey team.

As well as the regular, often weekly, meetings there were special events. Highlights in the early part of 1905, for example, included the following:

Date	Event
2nd- 4th January	Sunday School annual "Treats"- prizegiving & entertainment
24th January	Choir supper
28th January	Scripture Union tea
31st January	Sunday School concert
2nd February	Band of Hope tea
23rd February	Whist drive for CLB funds (by the Ladies' Working Party)
7th March	Church Lads' Brigade concert and prizegiving
18th April	Choir's performance of Stainer's "Crucifixion"
23rd April	Easter tea and entertainment

In the autumn, there was always a fund-raising Bazaar which lasted between two and four days.

Summer excursions were also a popular feature of the time. In 1905, the programme was as follows:

Date	Organisation	Destination
13th June	Choir men	Matlock
24th June	Scripture Union	Braunstone
10th July	Sunday School - seniors	High Tor Farm
15th July	Young Women's Communicants' Guild	Woodhouse
18th July	Mothers' Meeting	Nanpantan
22nd July	Sunday School - infants	Aylestone Road
23rd July	Choir boys	Cleethorpes
26th August	Sunday School - teachers	Beaumanor Park

With a population of over 11,000 (before the separation of All Souls'), not everyone in the parish was involved with St Andrew's but few can have been unaware of its presence. In addition, of course, there were other churches within walking distance and a range of Non-conformist chapels, most with a similar range of activities. In 1905, St Andrew's claimed a congregation of 700-800, with 536 Easter communicants. There were about 900 Sunday School scholars and 70 teachers. During the year, the Church conducted 148 baptisms and 69 marriages.

Chapter 4
1912 – 1962: Maturity

Shortly before Easter 1915, the Reverend Leonard Arthur Matthew became the eighth Vicar of St Andrew's. He was to be the first of three hard-working and determined priests, all in the Anglo-Catholic tradition, who together served St Andrew's for more than 70 years. In 1928, Fr Matthew was succeeded by the Reverend James George Gillman and, after 25 years, he was followed by the Reverend Bernard Badger. Fr Badger (always known as "Father Bernard") stayed for more than 30 years. Between them, these three priests dominated St Andrew's for most of the twentieth century. They created its distinctive ethos and reputation and are still remembered with great affection.

For about forty years, the continuity at the Church was matched by stability in the parish. There was little new building during this period and the close-knit community which had developed in the terraced streets was generally a settled one. A picture of life in the parish is painted by Colin Hyde in his oral history, "Walnut Street: Past, Present and Future", which brings together memories of the area from before the 1960s. In many ways, the community was self contained, with factories, pubs, a cinema and a wide variety of shops all in close proximity. For many people, family ties were strong and, although living standards were low, poverty was a shared experience and there was much mutual support. Most residents took pride in their homes and neighbourhoods and only a few localities were considered "rough". Fr Bernard later wrote of *"a close-knit, homogeneous artisan community with lots of character and vitality".[11]*

By modern standards, life was hard and precarious. For those in work, hours were usually long and conditions often poor. The situation was worse for those without work and, although Leicester fared comparatively well, there were significant and persistent levels of unemployment throughout the 1920s and 1930s. The presence of coal fires, factories and a local power station ensured that a dirty, smoky atmosphere often hung over the parish and, until the coming of the National Health Service in 1948, most residents

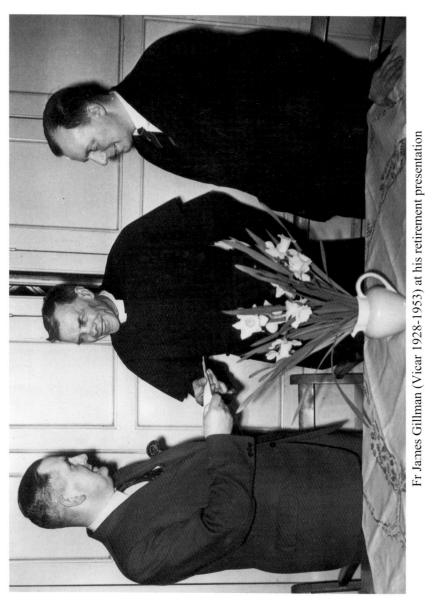

Fr James Gillman (Vicar 1928-1953) at his retirement presentation
with the Churchwardens, Tom Allen (left) and A.H. Tilley (right)

Photograph courtesy of the Leicester Mercury

struggled to pay for proper medical care. The 'community' embraced many people but the position of those who failed to 'fit in' was especially difficult. For everyone, this period included the trauma of two World Wars.

When Fr Matthew arrived in 1915 he was a comparatively young man and St Andrew's was his first incumbency. He had already served a curacy in Leicester, at St George's. Fr Matthew is credited with bringing Anglo-Catholicism to St Andrew's 'almost overnight'. This, as the previous chapter has shown, is an exaggeration but he certainly reinvigorated and developed an earlier tradition. On his first Sunday at St Andrew's, Fr Matthew ensured that the Eucharist displaced Matins as the principal service at 11am and, by his second week, he had instituted its celebration on a daily basis. By 1919, a "Church Times" survey also noted the use of Eucharistic vestments and incense at St Andrew's and the reservation of the sacrament. At the time, only two other churches in Leicester, namely St Paul's and St Stephen's (East Park Road), had adopted all these Anglo-Catholic practices.

In the same spirit, Fr Matthew quickly set about modifying the interior of the church to allow it to stage more frequent and elaborate services. Many Anglo-Catholics felt that the Church should be offering a 'glimpse of heaven', that its services should be providing colour, music, beauty and drama to lift people out of their drab and humdrum lives, especially in poor parishes. At St Andrew's, a new altar, decorated with mother of pearl and gold leaf, was acquired and was set on high at the far end of the sanctuary, topped with additional candles. A new three manual organ was installed at the west end of the Church and the choir was also moved there. This allowed the choir stalls to be taken out of the chancel and the sanctuary to be greatly enlarged.

The transepts were converted into chapels. The north chapel, dedicated to St John, was the site for a memorial to those parishioners who died in the First World War; it contains 104 names. The south chapel, dedicated to Our Lady, was intended for weekday celebrations of the Eucharist and is still used for this purpose. In 1927, its walls were panelled in oak.

Fr Matthew left St Andrew's in 1928 following medical advice and moved to London to become an Organising Secretary for the Anglo-Catholic Congress. A contemporary paid him the following tribute:

> *"Tall, well built, with a fine voice, and a magnificent organiser, his wise counsel and forceful personality were soon felt, not only in the Parish, but throughout the town, and St Andrew's was quickly in the forefront of the*

Catholic Movement. But he is probably best remembered by those who knew him as a visitor to their homes, a consoler in the sick room, and in the confessional."[12]

The ninth Vicar of St Andrew's, Fr James Gillman, was inducted in April 1928. He was the first incumbent to be appointed by the Bishop of Leicester (rather than the Bishop of Peterborough), following the restoration of the Diocese of Leicester in 1926 and the selection of St Martin's Church as the new Cathedral. Fr Gillman had spent a long curacy, including the years of the First World War, at Woolwich in south London where his church had a particular concern for the workers at Woolwich Arsenal. He first moved to Leicestershire in 1924 as the Rector of Peatling Parva, a small village near Lutterworth. The bustling city parish of St Andrew's must have been a sharp contrast but closer to his earlier experience at Woolwich.

Fr Gillman came to a Church whose Anglo-Catholic credentials were now well established. This gave him responsibility for maintaining a full programme of services throughout the week and brought an expectation that the principal services would be elaborate and dignified affairs involving the

Photograph: Robin Stevenson, 2012

The south porch and south wall, fronting on to Jarrom Street.

choir and a team of servers. The Eucharist (soon to be termed the Mass) was celebrated at 8am, 9.30am and 11am on a Sunday and this was supplemented by Evensong at 6.30pm. Although the Mass at 11am was considered the main service, almost all those taking communion would do so at 8am or 9.30am, encouraged by the requirement to fast for at least three hours beforehand. On ordinary weekdays, Fr Gillman would usually say Mass at 7am and Evensong at 6pm. On feast days, he would celebrate Mass at 6.15am to allow parishioners to attend before work. For individual parishioners, there were also services to mark significant stages in their lives such as baptism, marriage and death.

The Vicar was expected to support and encourage a range of organisations attached to the Church. In 1936, the Bishop was told that St Andrew's had *"a men's meeting, a women's meeting, Church Lads Brigade, Training Corps, Rovers, Scouts, Cubs, Guides and Brownies."* [13] In addition, there was a Sunday School on Sunday afternoons. The choir and serving team were large and included many boys from the local area. After Sunday duties were over, they were often entertained at the vicarage. (The lack of similar entertainment for girls is lamented to this day.)

St Andrew's influence in the parish was also felt through the Church Schools at Laxton Street and Deacon Street. The Church had some financial responsibility for these Schools and the Vicar was usually involved in their management and in teaching religious education. This was also the age when the clergy were expected to be visible in the parish and to visit extensively. There were other Church activities to be encouraged too, including missions, bazaars, whist drives and a monthly magazine. Even if local people had no other contact with St Andrew's, they would hear its bell toll three times a day – at 6am, noon and 6pm. For some, the noon bell was the signal to put on the potatoes for dinner!

Some families made St Andrew's the centre of their social as well as their spiritual lives. In a time when people rarely travelled and there were few counter attractions, this was much more common than it is today. A glimpse of how full life could be is given in the following account of John Allen's early life. John was born in 1927.

"John had a happy childhood and much of the first 18 years of his life revolved around family involvement at St Andrew's, Jarrom Street. ... John and Peter [his brother] were the third generation of Allens to worship there and both sets of grandparents attended St Andrew's from the early days,

along with various aunts, uncles and cousins. ... Fr Matthew and Fr Gillman were the Vicars of the day and it was Fr Gillman who was to have a big influence on John's early spiritual life. In John's younger years the family would either walk or cycle to church (a good mile or two) in time for the 8am Eucharist. This was followed by High Mass at 11am, family lunches with one or other set of grandparents who all lived in the Parish, Bible class and Crusaders in the afternoon and Evensong at 6.30pm. From a young age, John sang in the choir and Peter was a boat boy, carrying the incense. ... On saints days and high days, Mass was celebrated at 6.15am and the family used to cycle to these midweek services and then go home for breakfast before leaving for school and work. Apart from the liturgical year, there were year round social and fund raising activities which the family were fully involved in – autumn fairs, jumble sales, whist drives, dinners and dances, pageants and passion plays."[14]

Fr Gillman was a familiar and popular figure around the parish, instantly recognisable in his cassock and cape. Some were wary of his unprepossessing appearance but he was widely recognised as a generous man who would help his parishioners regardless of whether they attended church. There are memories of him interrupting a confirmation class to attend to a neighbour asking for coal, of his housekeeper putting a lock on the pantry door to prevent him giving away food and of him giving tuition to a local boy who had missed school through illness.

Fr Gillman is also remembered as a collector – of preserved butterflies and dragonflies, autographs, coins and postcards. His butterfly collection made a particular impression; *"I can still smell the camphor!"* exclaimed one parishioner more than 60 years later. Part of the collection was displayed in the Vicarage hallway and proved a useful 'conversation starter'. Fr Gillman had a great love of flowers and the countryside and would create hand-made Christmas cards incorporating pressed flowers. He sketched, painted and, in 1934, published a long poem entitled 'The Divine Journey'.

Biographers stress Fr Gillman's love of children and his *"stout defence of them if need be".*[15] Some advice he gave in the 1920s has a surprisingly modern 'ring' to it:

"Boys are wriggly creatures (I was, as a boy). ... If you see a wriggly boy [in church] don't pounce on him and shake him ... or even shake your fist at him. Go and sit next to him and let him look over your Prayer Book. You will find

Fr John Ruston (Curate 1954-1957) (left) and Fr Bernard Badger
(Vicar 1953-1984) (right) outside the Vicarage c.1956.

that the wriggler will cease wriggling and you will both enjoy the service doubly. "[16]

At first, Fr Gillman was usually assisted by a Curate (though never by the three Curates of earlier days). By 1941, however, funds were short and the current Curate was advised that the Parish would not be able to retain his services. Thereafter, Fr Gillman worked alone. He took St Andrew's through the Second World War and the years of austerity afterwards but retired in 1953, becoming an assistant priest at the Church of the Annunciation in Chiselhurst, Kent. He died in 1962.

At St Andrew's, Fr Gillman was succeeded by Fr Bernard Badger. Fr Bernard had been a Major in the Hampshire Regiment, trained at Cuddesdon Theological College and served a first curacy in Leicester at St Mark's, Belgrave Gate. His arrival coincided with a new sense of optimism and energy; the War years were finally over, full employment was bringing increased prosperity for many parishioners and an extended welfare state was providing a cushion against extreme need. The Church had a young Vicar who was soon to be joined by a Curate and the number of communicants was increasing. Within a few years, however, this world would be turned upside down as the next chapter will recount.

In the meantime, a controversial change was made to the interior of the Church. Scott's design for St Andrew's focused attention on the sanctuary as the place where the Eucharist would be celebrated. Subsequent generations had sought to emphasise this by increasing the amount of decoration around the altar. Stained glass was inserted in the windows, angels painted between the window heads, curtains and a reredos placed behind the altar and banners displayed around it. Some doubts about this essentially Victorian approach were evident as early as 1922 when the Diamond Jubilee brochure aspired to an oak panelled or colourwashed chancel. However, no action was taken until the 1950s, when the post-war reaction to Victorian 'fussiness' was at its peak. After restoring the damp-proof course and allowing the walls to dry out, in 1955, the sanctuary was painted over in pastel shades and most of the ornamentation removed. The chapels received similar treatment soon afterwards although the oak panelling in the Lady Chapel was retained. Now attention focused on the high altar, not because its presence was heralded by lots of decoration but because there was little else in the sanctuary to distract the eye. The change was not to everyone's taste.

Chapter 5

1962 – 2012: Survival

In 1962, St Andrew's celebrated its centenary. There were, however, dark clouds on the horizon and even the Bishop was guarded in his letter of greeting: *"The passing of the years has left St Andrew's with many problems that were not foreseen at the time it was built."*[17] It had become clear that the parish was at the centre of a huge redevelopment scheme. In part, this was the result of the City Council's slum clearance programme but it was given extra impetus by the wish of two public institutions, already established in the area, to expand. Both the Royal Infirmary and De Montfort University (as it was to become) needed far more space.

The original Infirmary site had been purchased in 1768. It was adequate for nineteenth century growth but, by the early twentieth, the hospital was beginning to 'spill over' into the surrounding streets. In the 1960s and 1970s a massive expansion took place, with the Infirmary's site trebling in size; it now stretched from Jarrom Street in the north to Walnut Street in the south and, in the late 1970s, even went beyond Walnut Street to provide blocks of flats for staff. Roads were closed or diverted and most of New Bridge Street, formerly known for its shops, disappeared beneath the new hospital buildings and car parks.

The original University building had opened in the Newarke as the Technical School and Art School in 1897. This building was extended in a modest way in the early twentieth century but, like the Infirmary, the University was to experience dramatic growth from the 1960s onwards. (The Colleges of Technology and Art combined in 1969 to form Leicester Polytechnic and, in 1992, the Polytechnic became De Montfort University.) The first major new development – the 10 storey Fletcher Building – opened in 1966 and the University campus was soon expanding in all directions. With its associated student residences, it now occupies almost all of St Andrew's parish north of Jarrom Street and east of Grasmere Street. In addition, an ever increasing amount of student accommodation is being

provided along Eastern Boulevard, whilst students occupy many of the remaining terraced houses.

The Council's slum clearance programmes were part of a national drive to improve housing conditions. Areas of old, unhealthy and over-crowded housing, lacking in 'basic' amenities such as running water and inside toilets, were demolished and their residents moved to modern housing, often in new estates on the edge of the city. Parts of Leicester were cleared in this way after the First World War and much of St Andrew's parish was tackled after the Second, starting in the 1950s. Many people welcomed the improved housing but others lamented the destruction of communities and felt that the "slum" description was often unfair.

Most of the cleared land was eventually occupied by the Infirmary or the University but some new accommodation was provided by the Council in the 'St Andrew's Estate', a development of flats accessed from walkways. This was not a success and, within a few years, it was replaced by 'low rise' properties in conventional streets.

Clearance and redevelopment produced a huge fall in the number of people living in St Andrew's parish. A population of almost 7,000 in 1950 fell to less than 3,000 in 1968 and to 2,000 in 1980. Similar falls also occurred in the neighbouring parishes. Not only were population numbers declining but the nature of the community was changing. Long standing family and friendship links were broken as people left the area. Shops and pubs closed. Doubts about the future discouraged owners from investing in their properties and areas of dereliction gave a strong impression of decline. The parish became an area of 'last resort' with new residents tending to be transient, with no connection to the local community. Fr Bernard described the result as *"an uneasy mix of people"*.[18] The vicarage was broken into on several occasions and, in 1977, Fr Bernard was assaulted by four intruders.

The redevelopment programme did not proceed smoothly but was subject to many changes of plan and timetable. In retrospect, it is easy to forget that a sense of uncertainty and anxiety hung over the parish for more than twenty years. An element of despair is evident in the Vicar's report to the Church's Annual Meeting in 1968, as summarised in the minutes:

Opposite: St Andrews amidst redevelopment. An unusual view of the Church from the east in the early days of the slum clearance programmes, July 1958. (Photograph courtesy of the Leicester Mercury.)

> *"Certain parts of the parish [have] occupied houses but it is mainly empty houses everywhere. New phases may not go up as quickly as we hoped due to the economic situation. Main effect has been the children. Weekday masses are still badly attended. It is difficult to keep the choir going. Also a lack of young servers. Organisations still keep going except for the childrens organisations."[19]*

In the same year, Fr Bernard wrote in advance of the Palm Sunday arrangements:

> *"Provided that demolition has not reached Deacon Street School by then, we will meet there for the Blessing of the Branches ... The procession to Church will, alas, be mostly past empty and derelict buildings, but we do this for the praise of God, and not to seek our own glory."[20]*

Clearance soon affected the Church Schools and the Knighton Street rooms. Deacon Street School closed in 1960 and Laxton Street School soon afterwards. The Deacon Street premises were converted into Church rooms for a few more years but, by 1968, demolition was imminent. The Knighton Street rooms, requisitioned for a British Restaurant during the War, were returned to St Andrew's in 1952 and brought back into use. They were demolished in 1972 to make way for the Infirmary's expansion.

There were changes too inside the Church, albeit less dramatic ones. An early act of Fr Bernard's at St Andrew's was to reorganise the Sunday School, moving it from the afternoon to the morning. The 1950s also witnessed the redecoration of the sanctuary and chapels, as described in the previous chapter. In the 1960s, the choir moved to the front of the nave, a shrine was created to Our Lady of Walsingham against the west wall and new stations of the cross were acquired.

The 'modernisation' of services took place in the early 1970s. Following the ideas of the Liturgical Movement and reforms in the Roman Catholic Church, the priest at Mass now faced the congregation and, at St Andrew's, it was decided to bring the high altar forward within the sanctuary. This allowed the celebrant to stand behind the altar and brought it nearer to the congregation. At about the same time, contemporary language was adopted so that, for instance, 'You' and 'Your' replaced 'Thee' and 'Thine'. These changes, combined with a dwindling number of choristers and servers, meant that services became less elaborate; in Fr Bernard's words, it produced *"a simpler, more home-spun worship."*[21] Gradually, High Mass at 10.30am became the service at which most people took communion. From 1971, coffee was provided afterwards to encourage the congregation to stay and talk.

Redevelopment of the area brought gains as well as losses. St Andrew's decided to use the compensation from the loss of Deacon Street School to build a Hall adjacent to the Church and to encourage its use by the wider community. Designs were submitted by the Church's architect, Roger Keene, as early as 1970 but negotiations over the amount of compensation and a land swap delayed the project. The Hall was eventually opened in 1978. Redevelopment status also brought access to government funds and they were employed to furnish the Hall, to provide staff to develop its use and, later, to extend it.

By the 1980s, the pace of physical redevelopment had eased and the area began to take on the character it has today. The parish which Fr Bernard left in 1984 was, however, very different from the parish he entered in 1953. It is a tribute to his commitment and resilience that he served it faithfully for over 30 years when he could have chosen to move to a more comfortable or prestigious position. It was no mean feat to maintain St Andrew's as a beacon of stability and hope during the long years of uncertainty and change. Fr Bernard's contribution was recognised in 1976 when he was made an honorary Canon of Leicester Cathedral.

Fr Bernard is remembered, in the words of one of his Curates, as a man of *"obvious holiness and dedication"*. He spent much time in the Church reading and praying but he was also well known in the area. (He was only seen without his cassock when gardening!) A shy man who could seem austere at first, Fr Bernard was a priest of warmth and humour to those who knew him well. There was much merriment in the "Robert Peel" after evening service on Sundays, on coach trips returning from Walsingham and on the annual carol singing tour of the pubs of the parish. Fr Bernard made a point of visiting all of the pubs at other times too, in order, as he said, to meet *"the other half of the parish"*. Parishioners remember his long, and sometimes plain-speaking, letters in the magazine; his ability to nurture priestly and monastic vocations in others; his decision (when the congregation was 'right') to say the mass in Latin; his devotion to Our Lady of Walsingham and his 'modern catholic' approach to church affairs generally.

In 1971, following some of the earlier Vicars of St Andrew's, Fr Bernard became a part-time Chaplain at the Royal Infirmary. He eventually completed 16 years of service there and is commemorated in the Chapel by a set of stations of the cross.

Photograph: Don Sherriff, 2012

Above: Fr Barry Naylor with members of the 'History Group' in the Lady Chapel, 2012

Below: The refurbished Hall. 'Christ in the Centre' passion drama rehearsals, 2012

Photograph: Robin Stevenson, 2012

Fr Bernard felt called to a monastic way of life but one lived in the 'outside world'. For many years, he was a member of the Oratory of the Good Shepherd, a small religious community in the Anglo-Catholic tradition. Members share a Common Rule of life and are committed to a daily pattern of prayer, celibacy and a simple lifestyle. Later, he was an Oblate of St Benedict and died whilst staying at Elmore Abbey, an Anglican Benedictine monastery in Berkshire.

Until 1982, St Andrew's was a separate parish with Fr Bernard as its only priest. For two short periods, he had the assistance of a Curate. Soon after arriving in the parish, between 1954 and 1957, he was joined by Fr John Ruston, another member of the Oratory. After leaving St Andrew's, Fr John worked for many years in South Africa and was eventually appointed as Bishop of St Helena in the south Atlantic. Fr Bernard's second Curate was Fr John Willett. He served between 1963 and 1966, shortly after the Centenary mission and in the middle of the clearance disruption. He spent much of his subsequent ministry in Peterborough Diocese and was Rector of Uppingham between 1982 and 1999.

Fr Bernard relied on close working relationships with his Churchwardens. Cecil Trory served for over 20 years (until he and his wife were tragically killed in a car accident) and there were substantial periods of service by Tom Allen, Terry White and Mary Watts.

In the early 1980s, a major effort was made to repair and improve the Church building. This was made possible by a substantial legacy from Eric Toller, a longstanding member of the congregation, and by the availability of government grants as part of "Operation Clean Up". All outstanding repairs were completed, including those to the bellcote. The chancel and both chapels were redecorated and new altars installed in the chapels. The organ was restored and enlarged (in part using pipes from St Matthew's Church when it closed). "Operation Clean Up" largely paid for landscaping works to the grounds and, most spectacular of all, for the re-pointing and cleaning of the exterior of the Church, revealing once again the colours and boldness of the original design.

In due course, the Church of England at Diocesan level sought to respond to the new situation in St Andrew's and the surrounding parishes. It did so at a time of mounting financial pressure when church attendance and clergy numbers were declining nationally. In the event, no action was taken until 1979 when there was a vacancy for a parish priest at All Souls'. At this point, Fr Bernard accepted the position of Priest in Charge, thus bringing it under

The May Festival of Our Lady of Walsingham, 1979: the procession.

the same leadership as St Andrew's. Both churches remained in operation, with All Souls' under the care of a Curate, the Reverend Alistair Baillie.

This was to be the prelude to a much more ambitious scheme. In November 1982, a new Parish of the Holy Spirit was created consisting of the parish churches of St Andrew's, All Souls' and St Nicholas', the Leicester and County Mission for the Deaf (to become the Church of the Good Shepherd) and the Chaplaincies of the Royal Infirmary, the University and the Polytechnic. Headed by the Archdeacon of Leicester (as Team Rector), the paid staff consisted of four Team Vicars, two assistant priests and three licensed lay workers. St Andrew's was no longer a separate parish but the Church remained open, with Fr Bernard serving as a Team Vicar and as Chaplain to the Infirmary.

At first, all the churches continued to operate but All Souls' soon became vulnerable when Fr Alistair left in 1983. It finally closed in 1987 and is now the Greek Orthodox Church of St Nicholas and St Xenophon.

Fr Bernard himself retired from St Andrew's in 1984. He continued as Chaplain to the Royal Infirmary until 1987 and then became an honorary assistant priest at St Chad's (Coleman Road), still in Leicester. He died in 1991, aged 75, and, fittingly, his body was returned to St Andrew's for the Requiem Mass.

After Fr Bernard's departure, there followed a period of almost 20 years during which priests stayed a short time before moving on, much as they had at the beginning of the twentieth century. At the same time, appointments at St Andrew's were increasingly combined with other duties in the Diocese. These trends placed greater responsibility on the laity to organise church life and to maintain continuity, the pressure being particularly intense during the 'interregnums' between clerical appointments. With falling numbers, the burden inevitably rested on fewer shoulders. For example, four members of the current congregation – Monica Clowes, Wendy Commons , Neville Iliffe and Mary Watts – have, between them, served for more than 45 years as Churchwardens.

The character of the parish also changed with redevelopment. The remaining residential areas did not, on the whole, become settled communities in the traditional sense. An Area Review report of 1978 noted that many of the new residents were *"of a very different character – young, mobile, single and to a very large extent concerned with living their lives outside the [area]"*.[22] The Church's concern for the parish continued but it was increasingly hard-pressed to maintain a range of activities and organisations as the congregation dwindled and fewer worshippers lived in the local area. A 'Parish Audit' in 1988 made a plea for *"more people, especially local people"* [23] and listed current activities as visiting the sick and elderly and organising a luncheon club, a cub pack and a Sunday School. It also noted the availability of the Church Hall as a local facility.

In contrast to the shortage of people, the financial position of St Andrew's had improved. The Toller bequest had strengthened the Church's own finances and the 'deprived' status of the parish could, on occasions, attract government and diocesan funds. In this way, St Andrew's was able to make building improvements and to sponsor paid staff to work in the area.

Fr Bernard was replaced as Team Vicar by the Reverend Colin Rushforth, a young priest from Lincoln Diocese. Works on the Church and Hall were completed and a number of organisations revived. Fr Colin stayed until 1987 when, following Fr Bernard's footsteps, he moved to the Royal Infirmary as Chaplain.

At this point, it was decided to appoint a new Team Rector for the Holy Spirit Parish and to nominate St Andrew's Vicarage as his residence. The Vicarage briefly became "the Rectory" but the Reverend James Bartlett remained in post for less than a year.

In his place, a new Team Vicar was found for St Andrew's. The Reverend John Packwood arrived in September 1989 and brought a long experience of parish and prison ministry. During his stay, major works were completed to the Church; the windows were restored (with the help of grant from the City Council) and the internal brickwork and roof beams were cleaned. The Church also sponsored Jane Brown to work in the parish as a Family Support worker, based at the Vicarage, and using grant aid from the Diocese and several other local churches. In addition, Don Sherriff arrived as a Reader.

Fr John left St Andrew's in February 1994 and, shortly afterwards, Canon Michael Ipgrave took over as Team Rector, using St Andrew's Vicarage as his base in the parish (although he lived elsewhere). He retained his position as Bishop's Chaplain and Advisor on Relations with People of Other Faiths.

A new pattern of worship was established. The main Sunday Mass at 10.30am was supplemented by weekday Masses on Monday lunchtimes and Thursday evenings. In addition, Evening Prayer was said on weekdays and there was a Sunday evening service once a month.

Fr Michael brought an international dimension to St Andrew's. Through his connections with Japan, he arranged for a Japanese couple, Keiji and Etsuko Maruyama, to serve as 'lay missionaries' in the parish for almost three years. Two Japanese bishops visited St Andrew's and a group of Japanese Christian students lived in the Vicarage for a time. On occasions, priests from India and Malta assisted with services.

There were enough fit members of the congregation to walk to Glastonbury on pilgrimage and to raise funds for a number of improvements to the Church. A loop and microphone system was installed to assist the hard of hearing and an area in front of the sanctuary was carpeted and cleared of pews. A large rood cross, from St Gregory's Church in Small Heath, Birmingham was hung above this area and proved a striking compliment to Scott's original interior. Outside the Church, a crucifix was erected on Jarrom Street. This was part of a joint venture with Holy Cross Roman Catholic Priory and commemorates three people who died for their faith in Leicester. It was dedicated in 1998, together with a plaque on Infirmary Square.

In 1999, Fr Michael moved on to take up a national role as the Archbishop's Council Advisor on Inter Faith Relations. He later became Archdeacon of Southwark and, more recently, Bishop of Woolwich. The Rectorship of the Holy Spirit Parish was suspended to allow a review to take place and there followed a long period of uncertainty. At first, St Andrew's received pastoral support from two priests on a part-time basis – Fr David Cawley, Vicar of St Mary de Castro, served as a Holy Spirit Team Vicar until 2002 and Canon Michael Banks, Canon Chancellor at the Cathedral, gave support between 2001 and 2003.

The uncertainty continued. With the hospital and university chaplaincies operating independently, the Holy Spirit Parish now consisted of just three Churches – St Andrew's, St Nicholas' and the Church of the Good Shepherd. By 2005/06, the Diocesan Directory listed only one Team Vicar in the Holy Spirit Parish and she was attached to the Church of the Good Shepherd.

The laity at St Andrew's worked hard to maintain regular worship during the interregnum which was to last almost five years. The pattern of three Masses a week was continued with the help of a great many visiting and retired clergy, co-ordinated by Richard Gill, one of the Churchwardens. St Andrew's relied heavily on such priests during these years and some, notably Fr Terence Byron, Fr Tony Jordan and Fr Michael King, still help on a regular basis. Very few weeks passed without three Masses being said. The Festival of Our Lady of Walsingham in May and the Patronal Festival in November were also celebrated, as before, whilst the annual service of blessing for animals and the Lent study groups maintained their place in the St Andrew's calendar. The church buildings were kept in good repair. Efforts were made to stay in touch with the local community by distributing occasional news sheets and by organising a monthly service at an old people's home.

Eventually, in February 2008, a new appointment was made to the Holy Spirit Parish. Canon Barry Naylor became Priest in Charge, taking on the new responsibilities (and those of the Abbey Parish) in addition to his existing roles as Urban Canon and Sub Dean at the Cathedral. To the delight of the St Andrew's congregation, Fr Barry moved into the Vicarage, thus restoring a clerical presence in the neighbourhood and maintaining the Vicarage as a place of residence. Visiting priests are still needed to cover some Sunday Masses but there is now continuity of pastoral care and leadership at other times and at most of the weekday Masses.

With confidence renewed, St Andrew's felt able to embark on a major project to refurbish the Church Hall and to provide it with a new entrance on Gateway Street. The completed building was dedicated by Bishop Christopher Boyle on St Andrew's Day 2011 and is being promoted as a facility for the whole community.

There have been other new developments too. The Church of the Good Shepherd has chosen St Andrew's as its new base following the closure of the Centre for Deaf People on Welford Road. Its altar and other furnishings were moved to the St John's chapel in 2011 and services for the deaf community and its friends are held there regularly on Sunday afternoons. Amongst the first users of the refurbished Hall was the "Presence Ministry", a 'café church' for people alienated by traditional church structures (and one of the Church of England's "Fresh Expressions" ventures).

* * * * * * *

After 150 years, St Andrew's still stands boldly on Jarrom Street as a witness to the past and as a symbol of hope for the future. A small but faithful congregation continues to celebrate Mass there three times every week. The services are less elaborate than once they were but the sense of devotion is no less real. The congregation is smaller than in the past but the support and fellowship it offers is no less genuine. There is no longer an array of organisations to join but there is a newly refurbished Hall available to the wider community which is already attracting new users. The next 150 years are full of possibilities!

Notes

1. Leicester Journal, 30th March 1860
2. Atkins, page 5
3. Leicester Journal, 21st February 1862
4. Leicester Journal 30th March 1860
5. Leicester Journal 21st February 1862
6. Transactions of the LAHS, Volume 2, page 90
7. St Andrew's magazine, January 1867
8. St Andrew's magazine, March 1908
9. St Andrew's magazine, January 1915
10. St Andrew's magazine, October 1900
11. St Andrew's magazine, October 1982
12. St Andrew's magazine, January 1962
13. Parochial Church Council minutes, 6th July 1936
14. Notes prepared by Marian Coom for her father's funeral, 2011 (by kind permission)
15. St Andrew's magazine, May 1962
16. Letter of 1927 or 1928, quoted in St Andrew's magazine, August 1962
17. Centenary booklet, 1962
18. St Andrew's magazine, October 1982
19. Church AGM, 12th February 1968
20. St Andrew's magazine, April 1968
21. St Andrew's magazine, June 1974
22. Area Review Team, page 5
23. Parochial Church Council minutes, 16th May 1988

This booklet has been written with the general reader in mind and detailed references to sources have been avoided. However, the author intends to lodge a fully referenced copy of the text with the Church and with the County Record Office so that researchers can, if they wish, follow up the basis of the statements he makes.

Vicars of the Parish of St Andrew's

1862-1874	John Spittal
1874-1885	Robert Guinness
1885-1898	Samuel Godber
1899-1900	Henry Tower
1900-1904	Frederic Llewellyn Deane
1904-1908	Frederick Barré Fiest
1908-1915	Alexander Sutherland Lindsay
1915-1928	Leonard Arthur Matthew
1928-1953	James George Gillman
1953-1984	Bernard Badger (Team Vicar from 1982)

In 1982 St Andrew's became part of the Holy Spirit Parish.

Main Written Sources

Books and Articles

Area Review Team (1978) *Tower Street/ Walnut Street Area Review; First report* (Leicester: Leicester Inner Area Programme)

Atkins, Rev E (1904) *Brief Account of the Work of Church Extension in the Town and County of Leicester 1851-1903* (Leicester: Leicester Archidiaconal Church Extension Board)

Badger, Bernard (1962) *S. Andrew's, Leicester; one hundred years of service* (Leicester: local circulation)

Brandwood, Geoffrey K (1984) *The Anglican Churches of Leicester* (Leicester: Leicestershire Museums, Art Galleries & Records Service)

Brandwood, Geoffrey K (2002) *Bringing them to their Knees; church-building and restoration in Leicestershire and Rutland 1800-1914* (Leicester: Leicestershire Archaeological & Historical Society)

Cole, David (1980) *The Work of Sir Gilbert Scott* (London: the Architectural Press)

Hextall, John Edward and Brightman, Arthur L (1921) *Fifty years of Church, Men and Things at St Paul's, Leicester 1871-1921* (Leicester: Bell & Co.)

Hyde, Colin (1996) *Walnut Street Past, Present and Future; an oral history of the Walnut Street area of Leicester* (Leicester: Leicester City Council)

Rimmington, Gerald T (2004) *The Oxford Movement in Leicester in the Nineteenth and Early Twentieth Centuries* (Leicester: Transactions of the LAHS, Volume 78)

Rimmington, Gerald T (2007) *William Fry; educational pioneer and Anglican priest in Leicester (1839-1877)* (Leicester: Leicestershire Historian, No. 43)

Simmons, Jack (1974) *Leicester Past and Present: Volume 2 – Modern City* (London: Eyre Methuen)

Sinclair Snow, WG (1952?) *Frederic Llewellyn Deane; Bishop of Aberdeen and Orkney* (Edinburgh: William Blackwood)

Victoria County History (1958) *Leicestershire – Volume 4* (London: Oxford University Press)

Newspapers and Magazines

Leicester Journal – especially 30th March 1860 and 21st February 1862.

Leicester Mercury – especially 23rd November 1881.

St Andrew's, Leicester Church Magazines – especially the Jubilee edition of February 1912, the Diamond Jubilee edition of October 1922 and Fr Bernard's letters in June 1974 and October 1982.

Unpublished Sources

Church AGM minutes from 1922; Parochial Church Council minutes from 1936; Rev Henry Tower's collection of posters and tickets, etc from the 1880s and 1890s; Registers of Services.